Architectural History

Nine hundred years ago a Saxon church stood on this site. Little is known about this early church and all that now remains is a carved cross shaft and the stone font.

The early Norman church, rebuilt in about 1140, would have been of simple cruciform lay-out, that is, with a central tower surrounded by a nave, a chancel and two transepts. The chancel would have had an apsidal (rounded) end. The north aisle was added soon after this, in about 1150. In 1190 the south transept arch and arcade were built and the south aisle added.

In about 1200 drastic alterations were forced upon the church when the tower collapsed destroying the south east transept wall. The wall was rebuilt, incorporating three lancet windows. A new massive tower was erected on the west end of the church, which was completed in three stages, and took a total of 300 years to build. In 1300 the chancel was enlarged to accommodate the increasingly elaborate church services of the time. The transept arches also had to be rebuilt as the new chancel was now five feet wider than the crossing. (Note the 'splayed' appearance of these arches in the ground-plan.) In 1337 a

is also at this time that the stone spire was added. It is recorded that the upper part of the tower had fallen, damaging the west end of the south aisle; the tower was rebuilt, and in the process given a spire. The south west pier was also rebuilt, the new pier being octagonal in section. The tower now contains a fine peal of 8 bells renovated and re-hung in 1986.

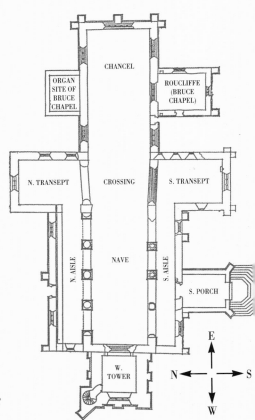

In 1407 a chantry chapel was added to the south side of the chancel, in memory of Sir David and Dame Margery Roucliffe. In about 1450 the nave was substantially altered, the walls were raised, the clerestory (upper storey) windows inserted and the roof replaced. Outside, the distinctive battlements were added. (It is more than likely that it was at this time that the wall paintings were commissioned.) These were the last major structural alterations made before the nineteenth century.

The nave and chancel

In 1806 and later some work was done to the roof as evidenced by the dates, and builders' names (F. Kirby & T. Grayson) inscribed on the crossbeams. Between 1876 and 1879, the church was put through a programme of thorough renovation. The north and south transepts were rebuilt and the box pews were replaced by the present seating. Finally the screen and vestries were added in the 1930s.

The Wall Paintings

Introduction

St. Peter and St. Paul, Pickering, is a remarkable church. It contains one of the most complete sets of medieval wall paintings in Britain. To step into this church is to step back in time. As we enter the 21st century and a new millennium, we can appreciate paintings completed over 500 years ago, and, with a little imagination, transport ourselves to the Middle Ages.

History

The wall paintings were probably first commissioned in 1450 and were painted in the following decade. Yet only 100 years later, they had been covered as part of the general process of the Protestant Reformation.

The paintings were first accidentally rediscovered in 1852, during restorations, when a thick coat of plaster was removed from the nave walls. Many people came to view the 'frescoes' at this time but they were subsequently covered again by a heavy coat of whitewash. It is known, from letters, that an argument about the paintings ensued between the vicar, Rev. F. Ponsonby and the Archbishop. Although the Archbishop appeared to approve of the paintings, the vicar felt that they were a distraction from his sermons and were full of 'Popish superstitions'. During extensive renovations in 1876, it was decided, by the then vicar, Rev. G.H. Lightfoot, to remove the whitewash, and restore the wall paintings to their former splendour. Further restorations have taken place over the years.

The Purpose of Wall Paintings

In the Middle Ages nearly all churches were partially or completely painted inside. However, this was not primarily for the purpose of decoration, or aesthetic enjoyment. The paintings were there as an aid to worship and to allow the largely illiterate congregations to understand religious stories. Indeed, wall paintings have been known as the *Biblia Pauperum*, or Poor Man's Bible. The scenes of martyrdom, often depicted, helped people in the Middle Ages face the closeness of death.

A Guided Tour of the Paintings

The tour begins with the figures of St. George and St. Christopher facing us as we enter the church, proceeds along the north wall of the nave to the crossing, and then follows the south wall of the nave, back to the entrance door, and Christ's resurrection.

St. George

George was born in Palestine in 280 and followed the profession of Roman soldier. He converted to Christianity and suffered persecution and eventually martyrdom in 303. The legend of St. George has been well known in England since the 8th century. St. George was an example of Christian chivalry and courage. He became the Patron Saint of England, the symbol of the eternal struggle between good and evil.

St George
Slaying the
Dragon

St. Christopher

*S*t. Christopher usually faces the
entrance to the church, as at
Pickering, in his role as Patron Saint
of Travellers. The legend of St.
Christopher recounts how a
young man, called Offero, set off
on a quest for the 'greatest
king' to devote himself to
that king's service. He
travelled the world
serving progressively
greater monarchs until, at
last, he found his way to a
monastery, there to serve
King Jesus. However Offero
knew nothing of prayer and
fasting, so the Abbot suggested
that he could serve Jesus by
carrying pilgrims and
travellers across the river to
the monastery.

One evening, Offero heard a
child crying on the far bank.
He took the child on his
shoulders, and was amazed to
find he was heavier than
anyone Offero had carried
before. The child said 'Your
load is heavy, because you are
carrying someone who carries
the sins of all the world'.
Offero was thereafter known
as Christopher - The Christ-
bearer. The painting shows
Christopher carrying the
Christ-child, with the Abbot
lighting their way to
safety.

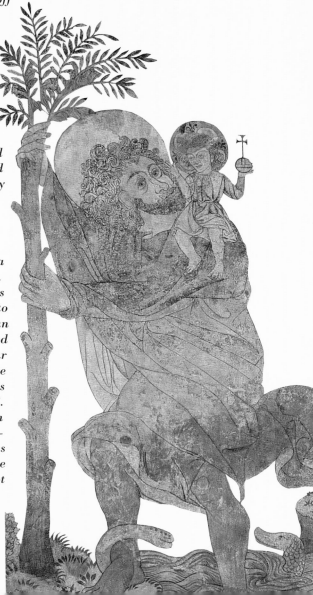

*Christopher carrying the
Christ-child*

The beheading of John the Baptist

St. John the Baptist

This painting illustrates the biblical story of the beheading of John the Baptist. On the right we have the haloed figure of the Baptist, who is telling King Herod that he should not have taken Herodias to be his wife. Herodias was the wife of the king's brother, and Herod was already married. Salome, Herodias' daughter, is dancing before the feast. Such was the king's pleasure that he granted Salome anything she wished. Not knowing her own mind, Salome conferred with Herodias, who told her daughter to ask for the Baptist's head on a plate. On the left of the painting we see the execution of John the Baptist and in the centre, we see the king again with Salome receiving St. John's head from him.

Coronation of the Virgin Mary

The painting of Mary above Herod's feast is probably the final scene in a sequence. The preceding three scenes are on the south wall. The crowning of the Blessed Virgin Mary as Queen of Heaven, follows her death, burial and assumption. A group of saints attend her, while at the top of the picture, angels, musicians and the host of heaven look on.

8

St. Edmund

*E*dmund was born in 840, and at fourteen he became the Christian King of East Anglia.

In 869 the invading Viking armies marched through Mercia and into East Anglia, destroying the abbeys at Peterborough and Ely on their way. Edmund was defeated at Hoxne on the Waveney. The Danish leader offered to set Edmund up as a 'puppet king' if he would renounce his religion and his God. Edmund refused. Therefore on November 20th 870, Edmund King of East Anglia, was martyred. He was stripped, tied to a tree, and shot with arrows and then later beheaded. The inscription on the right reads: 'Heaven blys to hys mede, Hem sall have for his gud ded'. (Heavenly bliss is his reward for his good deed.)

The Martyrdom
of Edmund

St. Thomas

*A*bove St. Edmund is a scene from the martyrdom of St. Thomas Becket. Thomas was a close friend and chancellor to King Henry II (1154-1189), who appointed him Archbishop of Canterbury in 1162. The King wished to bring the church under state control, and, having made Thomas Archbishop, he attempted to do just this. To his great disappointment, Thomas refused to co-operate. This argument lasted for more than five years. Finally, in a fit of anger,

Henry demanded: 'Will no-one rid me of this turbulent priest?' Four of Henry's knights, taking him at his word, journeyed to Canterbury to murder Thomas. This act shocked the Christian world. Pope Alexander III declared Becket a saint, and his shrine, in Canterbury, became the most hallowed spot in England. The painting shows the four knights in the cathedral wearing the armour of Edward IV (1461-1483) from which we can date the painting.

St. Catherine

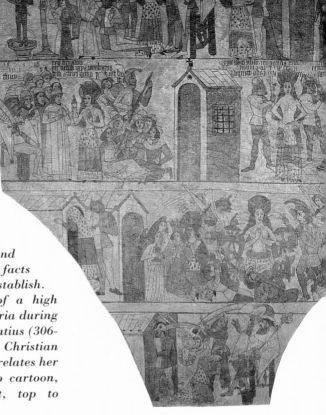

*O*pposite St. Edmund on the south wall is a depiction of the legend of Catherine of Alexandria. St. Catherine was widely revered; she became patron saint of women, virgins, philosophers and students. Nevertheless, the facts of her life are hard to establish. She was the daughter of a high ranking family in Alexandria during the rule of Emperor Maxentius (306-312). Catherine was a Christian convert, and the painting relates her legend (much like a strip cartoon, proceeding left to right, top to bottom):

1. *Catherine protests to the emperor about the worship of an idol.*
2. *She is put in prison.*
3. *She debates religion with the emperor's philosophers and converts them.*
4. *This so enrages Maxentius that he has the philosophers killed.*
5. *Catherine is brought out of prison, stripped to the waist and flogged.*
6. *She is returned to prison still defiant.*
7. *She is visited by the Empress Faustina who is converted, moved by the constancy of Catherine.*
8. *Faustina is executed, and Catherine tortured on a spiked wheel, which breaks asunder. (It is interesting to note that the popular firework, the Catherine Wheel is named after this event.)*
9. *Catherine awaits her execution, unrepentant.*

The Seven Corporal Acts of Mercy

*T*he Acts of Mercy are taken from the text of the gospel according to St. Matthew: Ch. 25, v. 35 - 37. The seven acts run as a band beneath the clerestory windows.

They are:

1. To feed the hungry.
2. To give drink to the thirsty.
3. To shelter the stranger.
4. To clothe the naked.
5. To visit those in prison.
6. To tend to the sick.
7. To bury the dead.

1.   2.   3.   4.   5.   6.   7.

The Virgin Mary

*B*etween the windows on the south wall are three paintings which concern The Blessed Virgin Mary. The first possibly represents her death with six of the apostles depicted. The second picture depicts the burial of Mary and the legend of the Jewish prince, Belzeray who, it is said, jumped astride the coffin and became fixed there. He was only freed by the apostles when he had fully repented. Because the third painting is so badly damaged its exact meaning may remain a mystery. However, it probably shows Mary's Assumption to heaven. The probable conclusion to the series, The Coronation of Mary, is on the north wall.

The Passion and Crucifixion of Christ

Following on from the Seven Acts of Mercy is Christ's Passion. Note that the vertical line in this band would more usefully appear between the Seven Acts and Christ's Passion, and not, confusingly, between the first two scenes of The Passion. Christ's Passion and Crucifixion are central to the teaching of the Church. The sequence is as follows:

1.   2.   3.   4.   5.   6.   7.

1. *Jesus healing the ear of Malchus, which St. Peter had struck off when the soldiers had come to take Jesus away.*
2. *Jesus before Pilate, the Roman governor.*
3. *Jesus is flogged.*
4. *Jesus carries the cross.*
5. *The crucifixion. Jesus' mother Mary, and the disciple John, stand beneath the cross.*
6. *The descent from the cross.*
7. *The burial of Jesus by his followers.*

The Descent into Hell

Perhaps the most striking painting in the church is the dragon's mouth, representing the jaws of hell or of death. After his death on the cross, and before his resurrection, Christ visited Hell to minister to the lost souls who had died without knowing him. The first to meet Jesus is Adam, holding an apple, the second figure is Eve. There are two demons in the background.

and Christ's Resurrection

To the left of Christ can be seen rays of sunshine, perhaps reminding us that, in the darkness of Hell, he represents the light of the world. Symbolically, this leads us to the final picture on the spandrel to the right – the resurrection of Jesus. The spandrel to the right of this scene contains a depiction of the resurrection of Jesus. A soldier falls backwards in amazement as angels look on at Christ rising in triumph.

Other Features of the Church

The Porch

*I*n the Middle Ages the porch formed a physical link between the secular and religious worlds. In the 14th century parts of the service would have been held here, and during fairs and festivals, stalls would have been set up in this space. Some early Norman carvings can be seen in the buttress on the west side of the porch. These carvings had previously been lying in the church yard and were incorporated earlier this century during renovations.

The Font

*T*he font is thought to be of Saxon origin, although the lower portion is of a later date. The slightly damaged condition of the font can be explained by an entry in the church registers, which reads: 'Baptisterii Pickerensis Demolitio, Septemb. 25, 1644'. It is possible that this event was connected to the battle of Marston Moor, which had occurred two months previously, or with the siege of Helmsley Castle, which fell to the Parliamentarians two months later. It is wonderful to think that those who are christened in the church today are christened in the same font that has been in use for a thousand years.

The Marshall Memorial

*T*his memorial commemorates the brothers John and William Marshall. In his day, William did much to advance agricultural practices. His chief publication was 'A General Survey of the Rural Economy of England'. He also proposed the setting up of a Board of Agriculture and this was eventually put into effect in 1743 by Parliament.

The Hepplewhite Pulpit

Capital detail

This carved grotesque can be seen on the west of the pier supporting the north transept arch, and probably dates from 1300 when the transept arches were rebuilt.

The Bruce Effigy

Just below the lectern, in the north east corner of the nave, lies the alabaster figure of a knight. He wears the mail and plate armour of 1340-50. The arms on the shield are those of Bruce. Since a licence was given to Sir William Bruce to establish a chantry in the church in 1337, there can be little doubt that this effigy is that of Sir William.

Many a sermon is preached from this beautiful late 18th century pulpit which displays the curves typical of the Hepplewhite style. Note the rich burnished colour and the intricate carved lattice-work around the top. The octagonal base is modern.

The Chapel
and part of the
screen

The Sedilia

The triple sedilia in the south wall of the chancel date from the 14th century. They have crocketed gables and four fine carved heads, two of which perhaps represent an archbishop and a parish priest.

The Chapel and the Roucliffe Effigies

This chapel, on the south side of the chancel, is where the clergy say their daily morning and evening prayers and is kept apart for private prayer. It was built in 1407 and contains the alabaster effigies of Sir David and Dame Margery Roucliffe. Leland, in his 16th century Itinerary, incorrectly identified the figures as those of the Bruces: 'I saw 2 or 3 Tumbes of the Bruses, wherof one with his wife lay in a chapel on the south side of the Quirr...'. The Chapel is, therefore, sometimes referred to as the Bruce Chapel. At one time, the chapel was divided into two floors and the upper part became a priest's chamber. In 1857 the floor was removed and the chapel was used as a school. The intricately carved door and screen are by Alfred Wilson of Pickering (1923).

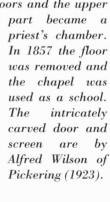

The American Connection

On the north wall of the sanctuary is a memorial tablet to Mary, Nicholas and Robert King of Pickering. Robert and Nicholas helped and succeeded L'Enfant in surveying Washington D.C. Underneath are brass plaques commemorating the Brotherhood in

Arms of 1917, and England's and America's alliance in the Red Cross, during the Great War. It is these memorials which place this church very firmly on the American Trail.

The creation
of Eve

Adam and Eve

The Reserved Sacrament (the consecrated bread and wine used for taking communion to the sick and housebound) is kept behind this delightfully carved door in the north wall of the sanctuary. The carving shows the creation of Eve from the rib of Adam.

St. Peter and St. Paul's church is Pickering's main link with the past and has been at the heart of its life for 1,000 years.

Consider the generations who have created, maintained and added to this building and marvel at the effort which they have put into this expression of the worship of God. Generations of Pickering's citizens have worshipped here, been married at the altar steps, have been baptised in the font and have had funeral services here. Remember also that it is not a museum. A vigorous body of worshippers and communicants attend weekly. This church is the Parish Church for Pickering and seeks to serve the whole community and to be 'there' for all who need its ministry.

Designed and Published by Heritage House Group Ltd.,
Heritage House, Lodge Lane, Derby DE1 3HE.
Tel: 01332 347087 Fax: 01332 290688
email: publications@hhgroup.co.uk

Text by Christopher Ellis with assistance from
David Callow and Francis Hewitt.

Photography by Peter Smith of Newbery Smith Photography.
Exterior Photographs by Peter Smith of Malton, North Yorkshire.

ISBN 0 85101 320 1

Vicars ...

1150	
13..	... ...on
1341	H. de ...aster
1349	R. de Queldriks
	R. de Pokelington
1388	W. de Laytingby
1568-1570	W. Coleman
1581-1600	W. Owrome
1602-1615	E. Mylls
1615-1659	E. Bright
1661-1690	R. Staveley
1691-1712	J. Newton, M.A.
1713-1740	R. Hargreaves, M.A.
1740	S. Hill, D.D.
1745	G. Dodsworth
1764-1768	S. Harding, M.A.
1788-1804	S. Harding, Jr.
1804-1809	W. T. Laye
1809-1814	C. R. Graham
1814-1857	F. Ponsonby
1858-1863	G. A. Cockburn, M.A.
1863-1875	E. Bennett, B.A. (C.-in-C.)
1875-1881	G. H. Lightfoot, M.A. (C.-in-C
1881-1902	G. H. Lightfoot (V).
1902-1929	Evelyn W. Drage, M.A.
1929-1936	Reginald A. Bundle, B.D.
1936-1947	H. P. H. Austen, M.A.
1947-1976	W. Wallis, M.A.
	Canon of York
1976-1983	H. Bates
1983-1994	G. Lawn, Canon
1994-	**Canon Francis Hewitt**